To Gordon —S.L.R. and C.T.

Acknowledgments
The authors would like to thank the following people and groups for their help with this book: Dr. Gordon H. Sato, Josette Gaudreau, Jack Hauck, Robert Gaudreau, Denry Sato, Nathan Sato, Sara Sato, Sue Sato, Stéphanie Paccard and the Rolex Awards for Enterprise, Tish Rosales and the Ansel Adams Publishing Rights Trust, Jesse Roth, AAAHLE, Nancy Patz, Sharon Cresswell, Olga Guartan, Jeff Cymet, and Marc Jastynne Collins. Special thanks also go to our designer, Christy Hale, and our editor, Louise May.

A portion of the proceeds from this book will go to support The Manzanar Project.

Library of Congress Cataloging-in-Publication Data: Roth, Susan L. The mangrove tree : planting trees to feed famililes / by Susan L. Roth and Cindy Trumbore ; collages by Susan L. Roth. — 1st ed. p. cm. Summary: "A cumulative verse, alternating with additional narrative, describes the ecological and social transformation resulting from the work of Dr. Gordon Sato, a Japanese American cell biologist who made saltwater and desert land productive through the planting of mangrove trees in the tiny African country of Eritrea. Includes afterword, photographs, glossary, and author's sources"—Provided by publisher. ISBN 978-1-60060-459-1 (hardcover : alk. paper) 1. Mangrove forests—Eritrea—Juvenile literature. 2. Mangrove ecology—Eritrea—Juvenile literature. 3. Sato, Gordon—Juvenile literature. I. Trumbore, Cindy. II. Title.   SD397.M25R68 2011   577.69'809635—dc22   2010034501

THE MANGROVE TREE

PLANTING TREES TO FEED FAMILIES

by Susan L. Roth

& Cindy Trumbore

collages by Susan L. Roth

Lee & Low Books Inc.   New York

By the Red Sea,
in the African country of Eritrea,
lies a little village called Hargigo.
The children play in the dust
between houses made of cloth,
tin cans, and flattened iron.
The families used to be hungry.
Their animals were hungry too.
But then things began to change . . .
all because of a tree.

This is the tree,
A mangrove tree.
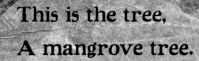

The land in Hargigo is dry and dusty.
There is very little rain.
It was hard for leafy plants to grow,
and the sheep and goats that eat leaves
did not have enough food.
Then a scientist had an idea:
to plant mangrove trees
by the shore of the salty Red Sea
so the animals could eat
the fat green leaves of the trees.

These are the trees,
Mangrove trees,
That were planted by the sea.

The scientist with the idea
was Dr. Gordon Sato.
He decided to plant mangrove trees
because their roots and leaves
help them live in salty water.
The roots stick out like pencils
above the water to take in air,
and the thick leaves squeeze out salt.
Mangroves produce seeds that sprout
while they are still on the trees.
These seeds become seedlings—
sturdy little plants—before they fall off.
Gordon studied how to make
the seedlings grow right by the sea,
in areas where the land
is washed by high and low tides.
Then he started his planting project.

These are the seedlings
That grew into trees,
Mangrove trees,
That were planted by the sea.

Most of the people who planted
the mangrove seedlings were women.
The project gave them a way
to earn money close to home.
To grow by the sea,
the seedlings needed extra nutrients.
Workers filled plastic bags with fertilizer
that contained nitrogen and phosphorus.
These are the nutrients that mangroves
would get naturally from rainwater
and streams created by the rain.
The workers punched three small holes
in each bag so the nutrients
would flow out at just the right rate.
Then they buried a bag near each seedling
along with an iron rod,
because mangroves need iron too.

These are the women
Who tended the seedlings
That grew into trees,
Mangrove trees,
That were planted by the sea.

The mangrove trees became
a leafy green forest
4 miles (6.4 kilometers) long.
Like all plants, mangrove trees
help the environment.
Their leaves take carbon dioxide
out of the air.
In exchange the leaves give off oxygen,
which people and animals
need to breathe.

These are the leaves
All plump and green
That wave in the trees
That grew from the seedlings
The women tended—
A forest of trees,
Mangrove trees,
That were planted by the sea.

The sheep and goats
gobbled up the mangrove leaves.
Gordon studied how much weight
the animals gained
from eating the leaves.
He decided they needed more protein
to grow bigger and have healthier babies.
So the goats and sheep were fed
a mix of mangrove leaves,
dried mangrove seeds,
and ground-up dried fish.
This mixture helped the mother animals
produce more nutritious milk
for their kids and lambs.

These are the goats
And these are the sheep
That eat the leaves
All plump and green
That wave in the trees
That grew from the seedlings
The women tended—
A forest of trees,
Mangrove trees,
That were planted by the sea.

Before Gordon started
the mangrove tree-planting project,
the village shepherds had to walk
into the highlands far away
to find food for their sheep and goats.
Once plenty of healthy food
was available nearby,
the animals lived longer,
and the shepherds saw their flocks
of sheep and goats multiply.

These are the shepherds
Who watch the goats
And watch the sheep
That eat the leaves
All plump and green
That wave in the trees
That grew from the seedlings
The women tended—
A forest of trees,
Mangrove trees,
That were planted by the sea.

Now the people of Hargigo use
every part of the mangrove tree.
Bundles of dry branches are fuel
for the fires that cook food
for the mothers and fathers and children.
There is more meat to cook
and more milk to drink
because the families own more animals.
The children are healthier.

These are the children
With dusty feet
Who play as the shepherds
Watch the goats
And watch the sheep
That eat the leaves
All plump and green
That wave in the trees
That grew from the seedlings
The women tended—
A forest of trees,
Mangrove trees,
That were planted by the sea.

Mangrove tree roots are hiding places
for many sea creatures, such as
small fish, crabs, shrimp, and oysters.
These small creatures attract bigger fish.
As a result, the local fishermen
catch more and more fish
for their families to eat and sell.

These are the fishermen
Who catch the fish
That swim in the roots
Of the mangrove trees—
Fathers of children
With dusty feet
Who play as the shepherds
Watch the goats
And watch the sheep
That eat the leaves
All plump and green
That wave in the trees
That grew from the seedlings
The women tended—
A forest of trees,
Mangrove trees,
That were planted by the sea.

Today Gordon dreams of mangrove forests
planted in many parts of the world.
He sees mangroves growing in countries
with seacoasts similar to Eritrea's,
such as Mexico, Peru, and Somalia.
He also sees mangroves in desert areas,
including the Sahara in Africa
and the Atacama Desert in South America,
where seawater can be pumped in.
The trees would help the local people
in all the ways that Gordon's project
has helped the villagers of Hargigo.

This is Gordon,
Whose greatest wish
Is to help all the fishermen
Catching their fish,
To help all the children
With dusty feet,
To help all the shepherds
Who watch goats and sheep,
To help all the women
Who tend the seedlings—

By planting trees,
Mangrove trees,
By the sea.

Afterword

Gordon H. Sato was born in 1927 in Los Angeles, California. He, too, was once a hungry child in a desert land. He never forgot his teenage experience during World War II in the deprived conditions of the Manzanar War Relocation Center, a concentration camp for Japanese Americans in the California desert. His family and many others were forced to live there, surrounded by barbed wire, because the United States and Japan were at war. To help feed his family in Manzanar, Gordon learned how to make corn grow in the dry, dusty soil.

Years later Gordon earned a doctorate degree and became a cell biologist. He first went to Eritrea, a tiny country in eastern Africa, in the 1980s. He helped fight famine there by raising fish for food during the country's war of independence against Ethiopia.

Gordon Sato (to right of sign) playing saxophone with Manzanar's jazz band

After Eritrea gained its independence in 1993, Dr. Sato wanted to help the people of the war-torn young country. Poverty and hunger were widespread. Dr. Sato observed camels eating leaves from mangrove trees that grew naturally in the country. He decided the leaves would also make good food for goats and sheep, which in turn would provide food for the people.

AFRICA

Eritrea

Camel resting near young mangrove forest

Shepherd with his flock

Dr. Sato noticed that mangroves could live in seawater in areas where freshwater streams, created by seasonal rains, emptied into the sea. He did experiments to learn which elements and nutrients the freshwater provided, and concluded that if nitrogen, phosphorus, and iron were added to seawater, mangroves could grow in it.

Mangrove trees growing in seawater

Women planting mangrove seedlings

Planting bag of fertilizer alongside seedling

When Dr. Sato began his planting project in the village of Hargigo in Eritrea, he trained a group of villagers to cultivate and use the mangrove trees. About one million mangroves have now been planted in Hargigo. Over time the trees have greatly benefited all the people of the village.

Young mangrove forest

Children playing in Hargigo

Dr. Sato has started two similar projects in northwestern Africa. He hopes they will be as successful as the one in Eritrea. In 2008, he began a planting project in Mauritania. The mangroves in Mauritania are planted 200 yards (about 183 meters) inland. Originally Dr. Sato's team irrigated the trees with seawater pumped in from the Atlantic Ocean. Then they discovered that the tree roots had reached down to seawater flowing below the soil, making irrigation unnecessary. In 2010, Dr. Sato began a new project in Morocco, planting two thousand trees to start, with millions to follow.

Dr. Sato with workers in field

Mangrove seeds

Hungry sheep eating mangrove leaves

Dr. Sato sees the Moroccan model as a way to create mangrove forests in the world's great deserts. He believes that large-scale planting of forests would have an enormous positive economic impact on world poverty and hunger. By reducing the amount of carbon dioxide in the atmosphere, the plantings could also help slow global climate change.

Mangrove seedlings in pots, ready for planting

Entrance to Manzanar War Relocation Center, 1943

The Manzanar Project is the name Dr. Sato has given to his work planting mangrove trees. Why did he choose to name his project after the concentration camp where he lived so many years ago? Dr. Sato has said that his work growing mangroves to erase poverty and hunger is based on his experiences growing corn in the desert at Manzanar. He wanted to turn those experiences into something good. He called his work The Manzanar Project to remind people that it is possible to fight injustice with hope.

Sign in Eritrea explaining goals of The Manzanar Project

Dr. Sato with men and women of Hargigo

New forest of mangrove seedlings

Dr. Sato has received numerous awards. In 1984, he was elected to the United States National Academy of Sciences for his work in cell biology. In 2002, he was named a laureate of Switzerland's Rolex Awards for Enterprise for helping to make the world a better place for humankind. And in 2005, Dr. Sato received the Blue Planet Prize given by Japan's Asahi Glass Foundation to recognize scientific work that helps solve global environmental problems.

To make a donation to help Dr. Sato and The Manzanar Project plant more mangrove trees around the world, checks may be sent to: Plant a Mangrove Tree—Feed a Family, The Manzanar Project, P.O. Box 98, Gloucester, MA 01931.

Young mangrove tree

Glossary and Pronunciation Guide

Atacama Desert (AH-tah-KAH-mah DEZ-urt): desert in northern Chile

carbon dioxide (KAR-behn dye-OK-side): gas that animals and people breathe out and that plants absorb during the day

Eritrea (er-eh-TREE-uh): country in eastern Africa bordered by Ethiopia, Sudan, and the Red Sea

Ethiopia (ee-thee-OH-pee-uh): country in eastern Africa

fertilizer (FUR-tuh-lie-zer): substance added to soil to make it richer and to help crops grow

flock (flok): group of animals, usually all of one kind, that live and feed together

freshwater (FRESH-wah-ter): having to do with water that does not contain salt; water that does not contain salt

Gordon Sato (GOR-den SAH-toh): American cell biologist who developed a method to grow mangrove trees in saltwater deserts as a way of addressing problems of hunger, poverty, and environmental pollution

Hargigo (har-GEE-goh): village at the edge of the Red Sea in Eritrea

highland (HYE-luhnd): area with hills or mountains

kid (kid): young goat

lamb (lam): young sheep

mangrove (MAN-grohv): type of tree that grows in shallow coastal waters and can live in salty water

Manzanar (MAN-zeh-nar): concentration camp in California where Japanese Americans were imprisoned during World War II

Mauritania (mawr-eh-TAY-nee-uh): country in northwestern Africa

Mexico (MEK-si-koh): country in North America just south of the United States

Morocco (meh-RAH-koh): country in northwestern Africa

nitrogen (NYE-treh-jehn): gas that makes up almost four-fifths of Earth's air; combines with other elements and is found in the tissues of animals and plants

nutrient (NOO-tree-ehnt): substance needed by plants, animals, and people to stay healthy

nutritious (noo-TRISH-ehss): providing one or more substances that keep plants, animals, and people healthy

oxygen (OK-suh-jehn): gas that makes up about one-fifth of Earth's air; needed by animals and people to breathe

Peru (puh-ROO): country in western South America

phosphorus (FOSS-feh-ress): element used in making fertilizers, matches, and other materials

protein (PROH-teen): substance needed by plants, animals, and people for growth; food sources for people include fish, meat, cheese, beans, and eggs

rainwater (RAYN-wah-ter): freshwater that falls as rain

Red Sea (red see): long, narrow body of water that lies between Africa and Asia

Sahara (suh-HAR-uh): desert in northern Africa

seawater (SEE-wah-ter): saltwater in or from the sea (ocean)

seedling (SEED-ling): young plant grown from a seed

shepherd (SHEH-perd): person who looks after sheep, goats, or other animals

Somalia (soh-MAH-lee-uh or soh-MAHL-yuh): country on eastern coast of Africa

tide (tide): constant change in the level of the ocean caused by the pull of the moon on the earth

Web Sites of Interest

The Asahi Glass Foundation, Blue Planet Prize
http://www.af-info.or.jp/en/blueplanet/list.html

Manzanar Mangrove Initiative
http://www.tamu.edu/ccbn/dewitt/manzanar/default.htm

The Manzanar Project
http://themanzanarproject.com

Rolex Awards for Enterprise (includes a video about Dr. Sato's work in Eritrea)
http://rolexawards.com/en/the-laureates/gordonsato-home.jsp

Authors' Sources

Aoyagi-Stom, Caroline. "A Love of Science Breeds a Life of Humanity." *Pacific Citizen*, November 21, 2008.

Cawthorne, Andrew. "Eritrea's mangroves show way to fight hunger." Reuters, May 21, 2008. http://www.reuters.com/article/idUSL19568436

"Gordon Sato: Transforming a coastline." Rolex Awards for Enterprise, 2002. http://rolexawards.com/en/the-laureates/gordonsato-the-project.jsp

Kennedy, Pagan. "Desert Saint." *Boston Globe*, November 14, 2004.

"Mangrove project creates fish, fire and hope in Eritrean desert." AFP/Terra Daily, April 14, 2008. http://www.terradaily.com/reports/Mangrove_project_creates_fish_fire_and_hope_in_Eritrean_desert_999.html

Pollack, Andrew. "A Drug's Royalties May Ease Hunger." *New York Times*, March 7, 2004, business section.

Sato, Gordon. Interview by the authors, February 6, 2010.

——. "The Manzanar Mangrove Initiative: An economic, incentive driven approach to end global warming." January 1998. http://www.tamu.edu/ccbn/dewitt/manzanar/default.htm

——, et. al. "A Novel Approach to Growing Mangroves on the Coastal Mud Flats of Eritrea with the Potential for Relieving Regional Poverty and Hunger." *Wetlands* 25, no. 3 (September 2005): 776–779.

Tan, Ria. "Mangrove Trees." Mangrove trees in general: info fact sheet, photos, 2001. http://www.naturia.per.sg/buloh/plants/mangrove_trees.htm

Teclemariam, Yohannes. "Manzanar Project: Eureka the Technique to Alleviate Poverty in the Barren Coast of Hergigo." Eritrea-Red Sea, June 8, 2008, last updated August 5, 2009. http://www.eritrearedsea.org/index.php?option=com_content&task=view&id=59&Itemid=26

Warne, Kennedy. "Mangroves, Forests of the Tide." *National Geographic*, February 2007: 132–151.